Acknowledgments

· ·

This book is dedicated to all of the weight loss surgery patients whom I have had the honor to work with and know. They have touched me with their genuineness, vulnerability, openness, and courage. I thank each of them for inspiring me, both personally and professionally. My hope is that others might be equally moved by their stories.

Please note that all names in this book have been changed to protect confidentiality.

The Weight Loss Surgery Coping Companion:
A Practical Guide for Coping with Post-Surgery Emotions

The Weight Loss Surgery Coping Companion
Tanie Miller Kabala, Ph.D.

Introduction

It is my pleasure to introduce you to the Weight Loss Surgery Coping Companion. Let me begin by stating that I admire your courage in pursuing this life-changing surgery, and I commend you for taking this important step in self-care!

I have the privilege of working daily with patients who have recently undergone weight loss surgery. Following surgery, these brave patients often experience a wide variety of emotions- emotions including loneliness, anger, anxiety, depression, identity confusion, and the overwhelming urge to overeat.

Many post-surgery patients tell me that they have never experienced these feelings before, or at least have not felt them so intensely, because they had previously used overeating to "numb out," "escape," "self-soothe," and simply "make the feelings go away." These patients frequently come into my office saying, "I have no idea how to cope without food!" This is why I created the Weight Loss Surgery Coping Companion. In this resource guide, I provide specific strategies, and help you develop personalized strategies, to enable you to cope with your feelings following surgery. I specifically address loneliness, anger, anxiety, depression, identity confusion ("Who am I?"), and the compulsion to overeat. My intention is that this guide provide you with strategies you will use not only following surgery, but for a lifetime. All the best to you as you embark on this journey of nurturing and self-care!

Very sincerely yours,

Tanie Miller Kabala, Ph.D.

Table of Contents

Chapter 1

Life After Weight Loss Surgery

"The psychologist who evaluated me before surgery said that the surgery could be difficult emotionally, but I had no idea just how hard it would be. As the weight started coming off, I was excited and terrified all at once. There were so many feelings, and I no longer could binge eat to escape them. Sometimes I just wanted to go back to my old life- hiding away from the world in my apartment and just eating."

- Carrie

What is life like after weight loss surgery? Just as Carrie said, most people find it very complex- exciting, terrifying, full of new opportunities, *and* full of new emotional challenges. What are these challenges? In listening to the stories of my patients, I've found that they fall into three broad categories: the challenge of adjusting to a new body, the challenge of managing others' reactions to weight loss, and, of course, the challenge of adjusting to a brand new relationship with food.

Adjusting to a New Body

Most of my weight loss surgery patients have shared that they've spent their entire lives overweight. Therefore, as Carrie said, weight loss after surgery can be simultaneously thrilling and terrifying; thrilling because of the "chance for a new life," and terrifying because of the new, anxiety-provoking opportunities it affords.

My patients frequently share that being overweight allowed them to "hide" from certain frightening experiences, such as dating, being physically intimate, making friends, and interviewing for jobs. As my patient Ginny said,

"I hid behind my fat all my life. Now that I've had surgery, I feel like I have no excuse not to 'put myself out there' and date. It's so scary. I have no idea how to date. I've never had a boyfriend....and I'm terrified of being rejected. I feel anxious all the time."

Just like Ginny, most of my patients report that having a "new body" means facing old fears- fears of intimacy, rejection, and vulnerability. In the chapters that follow, my goal is to help you cope with the feelings associated with your "new body" and the new opportunities it affords, so that you can "get out there" and live life to the fullest.

Managing Others' Reactions to Surgery and Weight Loss

Nearly all of my patients have shared that they have received "unique" reactions to their surgery and resulting weight loss. While friends and family are often thrilled about a loved one's weight loss, there are instances in which the reactions are hurtful, stressful, or confusing. Kate, for example, shared that her best friend became very envious of her weight loss. This led to a breach in the friendship and significant pain, anger, and loneliness for Kate. Another patient, Sara, shared the following:

"I realized that I'd always bonded with two of my friends around being fat together. When I couldn't overeat with them anymore, I felt really left out. They couldn't understand what I was going through."

Still another patient, Ginny, shared this experience:

"When I lost weight, my brother said to my sister, 'Now Ginny is the skinniest one in the family.' This did not go over well with my sister. Things are so tense between us now."

Hurtful reactions are unfortunately a common part of the post-weight loss surgery experience. In the chapters that follow, I provide concrete strategies for coping with the feelings that such hurtful reactions can spawn- loneliness, anxiety, anger, depression, and identity confusion.

Adjusting to a New Relationship with Food

Many weight loss surgery patients have a long history of using overeating as a means to cope with challenging emotions. As Vickie shared,

"After a hard day, I'd just come home, get in my comfy clothes, and eat fatty foods like macaroni and cheese and cupcakes. It was the only thing I knew to make me feel better."

Following weight loss surgery, patients like Vickie are faced with the challenging task of finding new, healthy ways to cope with their emotions. This can feel completely overwhelming. As another patient, Evelyn, said,

"Yeah, before the surgery, at least I knew what to do when I felt stressed-eat. Now, I have no idea, so it's like a double-whammy- I feel stressed out to start, and helpless to do anything about it, which makes me even more stressed."

It was statements like this that motivated me to write the following chapters of this book. In them, you will find concrete, personalized strategies for coping with all of the feelings that frequently accompany weight loss surgery: loneliness, anger, anxiety, depression, identity confusion, and the overwhelming desire to overeat.

I'm so glad that you decided to take this step in self-care with me.

Let's get started!

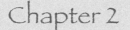

Chapter 2

How to Cope with Loneliness

"After surgery, I felt horribly lonely. Not only was I lacking in friendships and dating, but it was also like I had lost my best friend—food."

– Kate

Loneliness is an extremely common emotion among post-surgery patients. Many of my patients have made comments like that of Kate: that after surgery, they are not only dissatisfied with their social lives, but also feel as though they have lost the faithful and comforting friend that has been with them since childhood- food. Kate talked about her loss in great depth:

"I remember being a little girl, coming home from school after another terrible bus ride where the kids teased me. They called me "Kate the Freight," and loved to chant, "We hate Kate!" My parents were divorced and my mom never paid attention to me, so I'd just go to my room and get in bed with the candy that I bought with money from my grandparents. This continued all through school and into college, where I requested a single dorm room so that I could be alone and eat in peace. Things just cycled and I was more and more alone, away from people and hidden away with my food."

Like Kate, many weight loss surgery patients have a long history of loneliness. Some have experienced neglect and abandonment from parents and other family members. Others have experienced rejection from peers. Many have used food as a means to escape from these wounds—and have found themselves increasingly alienated from others in the process.

Perhaps you have had similar experiences. Perhaps you too learned to **survive** using food as a coping mechanism- a means of escaping from the pain. There is no **shame** in this- in fact, it is evidence of your **resilience.** As a child and/or adolescent, you did the absolute best you could under painful and challenging circumstances. Now, however, you have the opportunity to replace your old coping mechanisms with new, healthier mechanisms.

Let's get started.

Coping with Loneliness Exercise #1: Feelings Clarification and Expression

Use the next page (and feel free to use additional paper) to clarify and express your feelings of loneliness. Write down whatever you're feeling— you can write, draw, even make a collage of pictures expressing yourself. This is an opportunity to move your feelings out of your body and onto the paper, which can provide a sense of purging and relief. There is no wrong way to do this exercise—your self-expression, in any form, is exactly right. If you're having trouble starting the exercise, you might use these questions to guide you:

- What makes me feel lonely?

- When have I felt this way before?

- What words best describe my loneliness?

- Is there someone I am missing?

- What am I wanting and needing right now?

My Journal Page

My Journal Page

Coping with Loneliness Exercise #2:
Identifying Needs and Wants

Now let's take a closer look at the last question of Exercise #1: "What am I wanting and needing right now?" In my work, I have repeatedly noted the following phenomenon: that for post-surgery patients, the notion of making one's own needs a top priority is a foreign concept. Why? Patient after patient has shared that because their parents did not attend well to their needs, they feel that their needs do not matter. Many patients have also shared that they put the needs of others' first in an effort to win love and approval. Because of these dynamics, many of my patients have no clue what their needs are. One day, when I asked my patient Sara what she was needing, she looked at me blankly and said, "I have no idea. No one has ever asked me that before."

Perhaps you feel the same way- unclear about your needs and wants because they were not honored by your parents. Perhaps you feel as though your wants and needs don't matter and that others' needs should come first.

Please read this closely: this is absolutely **not** the case- you are a valuable person and your needs **do** matter- tremendously. No parent or other caregiver, under ANY circumstances, should make a child feel as if her needs are unimportant. If your caregiver(s) did this, **rest assured that this is not because of anything you did, didn't do, were, or were not—you were an innocent child who deserved unconditional love, nurturing, and attention.** If you were neglected, mistreated, or abused, it was your caregivers' issues that were the cause. I encourage you to re-read this many times if it's a new concept!

Now, let's get to work on making your needs and wants a priority!

Think again about your feelings of loneliness. What do you need in order to feel less lonely? Use the space below to express your needs and wants. If you're having difficulty identifying these, you might use these questions to guide you:

- Do I want/need to make more personal connections (friends, family, dating)?

- Do I want/need to find a community of which to be a part?

- Do I want/need support for my post-surgery experience?

- Do I want/need a pet?

- Do I want/need to call someone? Get together with someone?

- Do I want/need to get out among people, without the pressure of a one-on-one interaction? If so, where would I like to go?

- Do I want/need to reconcile an issue with someone in my life so that we can reconnect?

Now, on the lines below, write what you specifically need to reduce your loneliness (e.g., "Join the women's group at church," "Take that jewelry making class I saw online.")

_____

_____

_____

_____

_____

_____

_____

_____

_____

_____

Coping with Loneliness Exercise #3:
Taking Good Care of Yourself

Now that you've clarified your feelings and needs, let's pinpoint some specific things you can do to cope with your feelings of loneliness. I'll start by listing some strategies that my patients have found helpful. Then, we'll take a look back at your specific wants and needs to personalize the list. Place a star next to any of the strategies that appeal to you:

1. Engage in a nurturing self-care activity. Sometimes we feel lonely but don't have the energy to "get out there" and engage with others. If you're feeling that way, try coping with these feelings by taking good care of yourself. Try doing something that will make you feel cared for- take a bubble bath, watch a comedy, do some gentle yoga, take a walk in nature, read a book you've been wanting to read, or get a massage, facial, manicure, or pedicure. Send yourself the message, loud and clear, that you are a loving and valuable person. What are three nurturing activities that you would enjoy?

_____

_____

_____

_____

_____

_____

_____

2. Volunteer for a cause or agency that you believe in. For example, walk the dogs at an animal shelter, help maintain a state park, "adopt" a child through Big Brothers/Big Sisters, teach someone to read at an adult literacy center, visit with patients at a hospital, teach a Sunday school class at church, help kids with homework at a child care center, serve meals at a soup kitchen, deliver meals to shut-ins through Meals on Wheels, or give tours at a museum.

Volunteermatch.org and Unitedway.org are great websites for finding volunteer opportunities. Volunteering allows you to connect with like-minded people while doing something meaningful, and studies have shown that volunteering is directly linked with happiness. What volunteer activities might be a good fit for you? Jot down any ideas below:

_____

_____

_____

_____

_____

3. Join a support group. Many of my patients have fought loneliness by attending Overeaters Anonymous meetings, getting involved in post-weight loss surgery support groups, and joining therapy groups. You might find great comfort and connection in talking with others who have been through what you've been through. You can go to oa.org to learn about the Overeaters Anonymous program and to find a group near you. Also, your surgeon is a good person to ask about local weight loss surgery support groups. Finally, many of my patients have found online support forums, such as the ones at ObesityHelp.com, extremely helpful during their recovery periods.

4. Speak with a therapist who has experience working with post-surgery patients. A good therapist or coach will provide you with kindness and support, and will help you better understand your pre and post surgery experience. If you would like to find a therapist but are not sure how, please refer to page 63 of this book. There, I have listed a number of resources for finding a qualified professional.

5. Join a group that is a good fit for your interests. Affiliating with a group is a great way to address loneliness. Not sure what type of group would be a good fit for you? This is not uncommon among post-surgery patients. I have found that many of my patients have not had the opportunity to reflect on their true interests and passions- they have been too busy trying to avoid punishment or gain approval from others. To explore your interests, I recommend looking at Meetup.org, a site dedicated to helping like-minded people connect through small group meetings or "meetups." Browse the options with an open mind and see what appeals to you. There are meetup groups for just about anything you can think of- board game players, lovers of Broadway musicals, walkers, dog lovers, acoustic guitar players, vegetarian cooks, sci-fi lovers, French speakers, health and wellness advocates, etc. Even if you don't feel ready to join a group, exploring your interests in a non-judgmental way is a great place to start. What groups might be a good fit for you?

_____

_____

_____

6. Reach out to a family member, friend, or other loved one by phone or in person. If you have specific friends or loved ones whom you can call, write their names below:

_____

_____

_____

If you aren't able to identify anyone, you're not alone. I have learned that many post-surgery patients struggle with identifying "safe" others with whom to share their feelings. Frequently, they tell me that they "can't trust anyone" or "don't want to burden anybody with my problems." These feelings often stem from painful past experiences, such as being punished for expressing feelings as a child, or from being rejected for expressing emotions to a partner or friend. If you struggle with such feelings, I encourage you to enlist the help of a therapist. He or she can help you identify safe others with whom to share your feelings. I have found that when I help my patients identify safe others with whom to share, they are often pleasantly surprised by the warm reception that they receive. They also learn that self-disclosure (of both "the good and the bad") with a caring person builds connection and intimacy.

7. Get a pet. Studies have shown that individuals with pets report less loneliness and anxiety than those without. If you're open to getting a pet, think about what type would best fit your lifestyle. Many of my patients have greatly benefited from the comforting relationships they've developed with their dogs, cats, chinchillas, guinea pigs, turtles, fish, and even an indoor rabbit.

8. If you are a spiritual or religious person, join a church, synagogue, or other such organization. These can offer great opportunities to connect with like-minded others in either large or small groups.

9. Take a class. Make it something that you are genuinely interested in- and again, if you're not sure what you're interested in, that's okay- just engage yourself in a process of exploration. Imagine yourself taking a jewelry making class.... a dance class.... a yoga class.... a meditation class.... a cooking class.... a singing class..... a computer literacy class.... an acting class.... a calligraphy class....a photography class. These are all examples of classes that my post-surgery patients have pursued. What might you enjoy?

_____

_____

10. Journal. Buy yourself a journal that you find appealing and write down all of your feelings. Make this journal your friend in the post-surgery process- the holder of your thoughts, feelings, wants, and needs. Some of my patients have also benefited from sharing their feelings with other patients via online post-surgery forums. Whatever the forum, it is very healthy to vent your feelings via the written word.

Now, let's make your personal coping card for fighting loneliness. Below, write down all the things you plan to do to fight your feelings of loneliness. Include the items generated from your wants/needs list (on page 10) and the items that appeal to you from my suggestion list above. I have included five spaces, but feel free to include more:

1. _____
2. _____
3. _____
4. _____
5. _____

Now you have a tangible list of strategies that you can use if you're feeling lonely—Great job! **You're all ready to take good care of yourself!**

Chapter 3

How to Cope with Anger

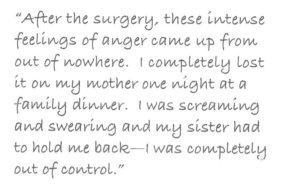

"After the surgery, these intense feelings of anger came up from out of nowhere. I completely lost it on my mother one night at a family dinner. I was screaming and swearing and my sister had to hold me back—I was completely out of control."

— Sara

Like Sara, many of my post-surgery patients are surprised to find themselves overwhelmed by intense feelings of anger. Because they suddenly can't use food to escape from the anger, it comes out FULL FORCE. They are confronted with intense anger towards their mothers, fathers, siblings, friends, classmates, uncles, aunts, cousins, grandparents, teachers, coaches, bosses, co-workers, husbands, wives, significant others, spiritual and religious leaders, and, unfortunately, themselves. They are angry about events both recent and distant   events from yesterday, events from 50 years ago.

In my work, I have learned that my post-surgery patients have very good reasons to be angry. Many have been seriously mistreated, both physically and emotionally, by people close to them. To make matters worse, many patients were taught that their anger (which was valid) was not okay. Sara recalled that her mother, who was emotionally abusive to her, shamed her anytime she expressed angry or sad emotions, often shouting, "Shut your mouth! You're a lucky girl and should be happy!" Other patients have come to equate anger with "being out of control," because their caregivers had anger management problems.

They therefore have come to suppress their angry feelings- to keep from losing control themselves.

Have you experienced this as well? Do you have a lot of anger inside? Were you raised to feel that it was not acceptable for you to be angry? Were you raised to be afraid of anger? If so, take heart. You are not alone, and we can address this together. Please hear me out on this: **it is okay to be angry- anger is a normal, healthy, and adaptive emotion.** Our goal is to help you understand your anger, recognize that it's okay to feel it, and identify healthy strategies for expressing and coping with it.

Let's get started.

Coping with Anger Exercise #1:
Feelings Clarification and Expression

As we did with your feelings of loneliness, use the next page (and feel free to use additional paper) to clarify and express your feelings of anger. Feel free to express anything you're feeling. Again, you can write, draw, make a collage of pictures, or express yourself in any other way that feels right. This is another opportunity to move your feelings out of your body and onto the paper, which often provides a sense of purging and relief. Remember, there is no wrong way to do this exercise. Your self-expression, in any form, is exactly right. If you're having trouble starting the exercise, you might use these questions to guide you:

- At whom am I angry? Why?
  What would I like to say to him/her/them?

- When have I been angry in the past?

- What words best describe my anger?

- Where do I feel the anger in my body?

- How has anger been handled in my family?

- What do I feel like doing with this anger?

My Journal Page

My Journal Page

Coping with Anger Exercise #2:
Reflecting on Your Needs

Just as we did with your feelings of loneliness, let's take some time to determine what you need in order to cope with your angry feelings. It may be very difficult for you to figure this out. As I've mentioned, many of my post-surgery patients have not been taught to focus on their own needs. If you're having trouble determining your needs, use these questions as a guide:

- Do I need to "get my feelings out" somehow?

- Do I need to express my anger to someone? At someone?

- Would it feel good to vent my feelings physically- for example by screaming, punching something safe, or running?

- Do I need to take myself out of a relationship that perpetuates feelings of anger (e.g., a relationship in which I am taken advantage of or abused)?

- Do I need to take myself out of a situation that perpetuates feelings of anger (e.g., a situation where I am not appreciated)?

Now, on the lines below, do your best to write what you specifically need to manage your anger in a healthy way. For example, "Stop babysitting for June unless she starts paying me," "Take that self-defense class I've been thinking about."

_____

_____

_____

_____

_____

_____

_____

_____

Coping with Anger Exercise #3:
Identifying Specific Strategies

Once again, now that you've clarified your feelings and needs, let's pinpoint some specific things you can do to cope with your feelings of anger. To start, I'll list some strategies that my patients have found helpful. We'll also take a look back at your specific wants and needs to personalize the list. Place a star next to any of the strategies that appeal to you:

1. Vent your anger physically. Many of my patients have found this to be very helpful. One patient hung a punching bag in her garage and uses it whenever she needs to vent anger in a healthy way. Others have opted to take self-defense classes like Tae Kwon Do, Karate, and RAD (Rape Aggression Defense). Such classes not only allow you to vent your feelings, but also help you develop physical strength and feelings of empowerment and control. Engaging in other forms of exercise, such as walking, running, yoga, or biking, can also help in the coping process. Be sure to consult your doctor before engaging in one of these activities, especially if your surgery was very recent or if you have other health issues. What physical means of venting your anger might work for you?

_____

_____

_____

_____

2. Express your anger through art. It can be incredibly healing to vent your anger through painting, drawing, dancing, or singing. One of my patients finds it helpful to get in her car, turn up the volume on a meaningful song, and sing at the top of her lungs. Another finds a movement class called "Shake Your Soul" very powerful. Others have found it helpful to paint, sculpt, and draw to express themselves. List below any artistic means of expressing anger that appeal to you:

_____

_____

_____

3. Write a letter to someone with whom you're angry. You don't have to send the letter (this is something that you could explore with a therapist) but just getting your feelings out can be very therapeutic. I frequently find that my patients keep their angry feelings inside, rather than directing them "out where they belong." This can lead to depression, anxiety, and fatigue. What feelings might you be turning inwards? Write them down below, along with the names of anyone to whom you would like to write a letter:

_____

_____

_____

_____

4. Vent your feelings verbally to someone supportive and caring. This might be a therapist (and tips for finding a therapist can be found on page 63), friend, family member, partner, or religious/spiritual leader. To whom might you like to vent your feelings?

_____

_____

_____

_____

5. Consider addressing the person or situation that is at the root of your anger. This can be extremely helpful, as it can provide a sense of empowerment, control, and, importantly, closure. Such a step can be very scary and complicated though, so I recommend exploring this with a therapist. He or she can help you clarify your feelings, explore options, and determine likely consequences.

6. Journal. As with your feelings of loneliness, I encourage you to buy yourself a journal and use it to express your angry feelings. Don't hold back! Write whatever comes to mind, moving the feelings out of your body and onto the paper.

7. Have a ceremony. As I mentioned earlier, many of my patients have good reason to be angry at people who have mistreated them or are currently mistreating them. Some of these patients have found it very therapeutic to have a ceremony in which they rid themselves of objects symbolic of a person or relationship that has been harmful. One client had a ceremonial burning of her father's shoes since they reminded her of his angry footsteps. Another burned all pictures and letters of an ex who had abused her. Still another had a ceremonial "pouring" in which she poured alcohol down a drain, symbolic of putting her mother's alcoholism behind her. All found that these ceremonies were empowering and left them feeling less angry. What kind of ceremony might be empowering to you?

_____

_____

_____

8. Breathe. Deep breathing, meditation, and yoga breath work can be very helpful in coping with strong feelings such as anger. Consider taking a meditation or yoga class, or doing a meditation, yoga, or deep breathing DVD.

If you don't have time to take a full class or do an entire DVD on a given day, I encourage you to take whatever time you can carve out (even five minutes) to do some basic breath work. Two examples of simple breath work that you can do anytime and anywhere are:

> **a. I am relaxed.** For this breath work, sit comfortably, close your eyes, and breathe in and out normally. On your inhale, recite, "I am…" and on your exhale, recite, "relaxed." You may use any other mantra that is meaningful to you. Some mantras my clients have used are, "Healing in (on the inhalation)…… pain out (on the exhalation)," and "Love in (to self)…… love out (to others)."

> **b. Breath attention.** For this practice, sit comfortably, close your eyes, and breathe in and out normally. Simply pay attention to your breath. Note where you feel the breath in your body. Do you feel it filling your lungs? Do you feel it in your belly? Leaving your nostrils? Whenever your mind wanders, just return to attending to your breath.

Now, let's make your personal coping card for addressing anger. Below, write down all of the strategies that you can use to cope with anger in a healthy way. Include the items generated from your wants/needs list (page 19) and any items that appeal to you from my suggestion list. I have included five spaces, but feel free to include more.

1. _____

2. _____

3. _____

4. _____

5. _____

Now you have a tangible list of strategies that you can use if you're feeling angry—great work!

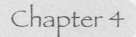

Chapter 4

How to Cope with Anxiety

"After the surgery, I felt extremely agitated and stressed. I was anxious about so many things, especially the possibility of dating for the first time ever. I just didn't know what to do without food to help me relax."

— Sara

Much like Sara, John arrived at my office overwhelmed with anxiety. He talked at length about how soothing and comforting food had been to him since adolescence- and how difficult it was to de-stress without it. John recalled coming from home from middle school each day (where he "felt like an outsider"), sitting on the couch, turning on the TV, and eating "everything: peanut butter and jelly crackers, chips, Little Debbies, soda, and chocolate milk." "It was how I relaxed," he said. John continued this behavior into adulthood, leaving stressful meetings at work and "going straight to Dunkin' Donuts for coffee and a half dozen donuts." After his LAP-BAND surgery, John found himself at a loss as to how to cope with anxiety without overeating.

Perhaps you feel like John- full of anxiety and unsure how to cope without food. Again, trust me when I say that you are not alone. Many post surgery patients struggle with anxiety- anxiety about how others will respond to their weight loss, anxiety about new experiences such as dating, and anxiety about "typical" things such as work, school, finances, and relationships. Rest assured that you can learn to cope in more healthy ways. **Let's get started.**

Coping with Anxiety Exercise #1:
What Feelings Are Underlying Your Anxiety?

In my work as a clinical psychologist, I have learned that a patient's anxiety often reflects the fact that she is struggling with **many** difficult feelings all at one time. Vickie, for example, came to me feeling very anxious after her surgery. Our work revealed that she was worried about losing her job, worried that she would "gain all the weight back," and worried that she would never marry and "would be alone forever." She was also very angry at her mother and sister, as well as a friend who had betrayed her. All of these feelings, several of which she'd been unaware, were "like a tangled knot of anxiety in my stomach." Uncovering these feelings gave Vickie a sense of self-understanding and control- and provided direction for the work that we would do together.

What thoughts and feelings might be underlying your anxiety? Is there fear? Anger? Disappointment? Guilt? Write them down below. Do not censor your words- just allow them to flow naturally, out of your body and onto the paper:

_____

_____

_____

_____

_____

_____

_____

_____

_____

_____

_____

_____

_____

My Journal Page

My Journal Page

Now that you have identified some of the feelings underlying your anxiety, I encourage you to consider talking with a therapist about them (again, tips for finding a therapist can be found on page 63). He or she can help you explore, process, and address them in healthy ways. To give an example, I helped Vickie identify why she is angry at her mother, encouraged her to vent her feelings in our sessions, helped her set healthy boundaries, and provided her with effective communication techniques to use within the relationship. We did similar work with the other issues that were causing her anxiety.

Coping with Anxiety Exercise #2:
Reflecting on What You Need

As with your feelings of loneliness and anger, let's take some time to determine what you personally need in order to reduce your anxiety. Again, it may be very difficult for you to determine this, as you may not have been taught to focus on your own needs. If you're having difficulty, use these questions as a guide:

- Do I need to take time to relax my body and/or my mind?

- Do I need to slow down?

- Do I need to simplify?

- Do I need support? From whom?

- Do I need to extricate myself from an anxiety-provoking situation or relationship?

- Do I need to take some things off of my plate?

- Do I need to say no to something or somebody?

Now, do your best to write below what you specifically need to reduce your anxiety (e.g., "Sign up for that yoga class at the YMCA," "Step down from one of the committees I'm on at the community center.")

_____

_____

_____

Coping with Anxiety Exercise #3:
Pinpointing Specific Strategies

Now, let's pinpoint some more specific things you can do to cope with your anxiety. Again, I'll list some strategies that my patients have found helpful. Then, we'll take a look back at your specific needs to personalize the list.

Place a star next to any of the following strategies that appeal to you:

1. Do some breath work, such as deep breathing exercises, meditation, or yoga. For centuries, these practices have been used to help us feel more relaxed, focused, and centered. Recent research yields strong evidence that when used regularly, they are very successful at treating anxiety and promoting a sense of well-being. You might consider signing up for a yoga or meditation class; or trying a meditation, yoga, or deep breathing DVD or CD.

Again, if you don't have time to take a full class or do an entire DVD on a given day, I encourage you to take whatever time you can find- even just five minutes- to do some basic breath work. Two examples of simple breath work that you can do anytime and anywhere are:

> **a. I am relaxed.** For this breath work, sit comfortably, close your eyes, and breathe in and out normally. On your inhale, recite, "I am…" and on your exhale, recite, "relaxed." You may use any other mantra that is meaningful to you. As I mentioned earlier, some mantras that my patients use are "Healing in (on inhalation)….. pain out (on exhalation)" and "Love in (to self)…… love out (to others)."

> **b. Breath attention.** For this practice, sit comfortably, close your eyes, and breathe in and out normally. Simply pay attention to your breath. Note where you feel the breath in your body. Do you feel it filling your lungs? Do you feel it in your belly? Leaving your nostrils? Whenever your mind wanders, just return to attending to your breath.

2. Blow off some steam. Exercise is a great way to manage anxiety. With your doctor's approval, consider walking, biking, dancing, jogging, swimming, kickboxing, or doing any other form of exercise. Try whatever appeals to you, as all forms of exercise help reduce anxious energy. What are some types of exercises that might help you?

_____

_____

_____

3. Clarify, vent, and address your feelings with a supportive person. As mentioned earlier, I've found that anxiety often results from having many feelings weighing upon you simultaneously. If you feel that many emotions are weighing upon you, I strongly encourage you to work with a therapist. He or she can help you identify and clarify your feelings, problem solve, and make action plans.

4. Consider addressing any situation that is contributing to your anxiety. Julie, one of my patients, recognized through our work together that her relationship with her mother was causing her tremendous anxiety. She shared that her mother had always been very critical and harsh with her (especially about her weight) and that "I just can't relax when I'm with her- I know she's judging me." We discussed ways that she could set healthy boundaries and protect herself from this anxiety-provoking relationship. She learned to "say no" to her mother, limit their interactions, and assert herself when criticized. According to Julie, these boundaries "made me feel more in control and way less anxious."

Some of my other patients have changed jobs upon recognizing the inordinate amount of anxiety their work situation was causing. Still others have addressed anxiety-provoking romantic relationships. What relationships and/or situations are causing you anxiety? How might you address them in ways that would reduce your anxiety? Write your thoughts below. If this is hard to determine, I encourage you to consider talking with a therapist.

_____

_____

_____

_____

_____

5. Say "no" when you need to. Many of my post-surgery patients find it difficult to say no. Why? As my patient Gina put it, "I want to be liked and am afraid of disappointing people." Gina recently recognized that she was overextending herself at church, "stressing myself out" with several leadership positions because she wanted to be liked by the pastor and church members. Through our work together, Gina addressed her feelings of "wanting to be liked," discovered activities that are truly fulfilling to her, and found the courage to step down from one of her church posts. Are you overcommitted right now? If so, take a few moments to reflect on what would feel good to let go of. What could you say no to right now? How might you go about doing that?

_____

_____

_____

6. Engage in soothing, self-nurturing activities. I've found that one of the best ways to curb anxiety is to slow down and take care of yourself. As I've mentioned, this is a foreign concept to many of my post-surgery patients. Is it a foreign concept to you? If so, I encourage you to reflect on what might feel soothing to you. Would a massage (or simply sitting in a massage chair) feel good? How about a warm bath, complete with bubble bath, candles, and relaxing music? Would it feel relaxing to read a good book or magazine with a cup of tea? How about a nice walk in nature? Would you enjoy purchasing a bird feeder and watching the birds outside? Take a few moments to think: "What would feel soothing and relaxing to me?" and write your ideas down below.

_____

_____

_____

_____

7. Do a Progressive Muscle Relaxation (PMR) exercise. PMR is a wonderful stress-relief technique that involves sitting or lying comfortably and then contracting and relaxing the major muscle groups, one after another. This technique is so relaxing for the body and mind that I've actually had patients fall asleep when we've done it in my office! I have included a do-it-yourself PMR script on page 65 of the Appendix. PMR DVDs and CDs are also available at most major bookstores and at Amazon.com.

Now, let's make your personal coping card for managing anxiety. Below, write down all of the things that you can do to reduce your anxious feelings. Include the items generated from your needs list and any items that appeal to you from my suggestion list. I have included five spaces, but feel free to list more:

1. _____

2. _____

3. _____

4. _____

5. _____

   Way to go: you're now prepared to cope when you're feeling anxious. **Great work!**

Chapter 5

How to Cope with Depression

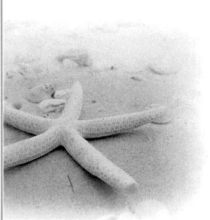

"Before I got the surgery, I thought it was going to change everything. You know—make me totally happy. But after the surgery, I realized that although weight was coming off, I was still the same person inside—still lonely, still unhappy. This made me totally depressed. I didn't want to get out of bed."

–Jean

Many patients confront depression at some point in their post-surgery process. Some, like Jean, are deeply saddened to find that the surgery has not provided speedy relief from all their troubles. Others, like my patient Shannon, experience depression because the "comforting indulgence of food is no longer an option." Still others have struggled with depression all of their lives. As I previously mentioned, many weight loss surgery patients have complicated and painful histories- histories including neglect, abuse, alienation, loneliness, rejection, and abandonment. "I've always had bouts of depression," Sara said during our first meeting, "Now I'm just a depressed person who weighs less."

Are you going through a bout of depression right now? Have you experienced depression in the past? If so, you are not alone. Nearly all of my patients have experienced some level of depression at some point in their post-surgery process. The great news is that you've gotten this book and are taking steps to care for yourself. Depression is highly treatable. **Let's get started.**

Coping with Depression Exercise #1:
Harnessing Resources

Before we design your personalized coping strategy, I would be remiss not to say a few words about depression and its treatment. Just like the commercial says, depression is a serious medical condition. Symptoms of depression include feelings of sadness, emptiness, or hopelessness; sleep disturbance; appetite disturbance; loss of pleasure in previously enjoyed activities; fatigue; difficulty concentrating; agitation; and suicidal thoughts.

If you are experiencing any of these symptoms, I encourage you to consult with a medical doctor and/or psychologist. These individuals can help you determine if you are experiencing a depressive episode and explore treatment options with you. As I've mentioned earlier, resources for finding a therapist can be found on page 63. You can also speak with your general practitioner (family doctor) or a psychiatrist.

Coping with Depression Exercise #2:
Pinpointing Specific Strategies

1. Move your body. Exercise has the immediate physiological effect of improving mood via the release of endorphins. Although it may be the absolute last thing you feel like doing, I strongly encourage you to engage in some form of exercise if you are experiencing depression. With your doctor's approval, take a brisk walk, do an exercise DVD, turn on your favorite upbeat CD and dance around the room, swim, turn on a fitness channel and try an exercise program (Gilad's Body In Motion is my personal favorite), take a class, or engage in any form of physical activity that appeals to you (or is at least tolerable). A psychiatrist once said to me, "After therapy and medication, exercise is the single best thing you can do to relieve depression."

If you're having trouble getting motivated, really try to focus on how you'll feel when you're done. Also, if you're comfortable, enlist the help of a loved one to help motivate you. As Suzanne said, "I just couldn't get up the motivation to exercise on my own. I used to call my friend and say, 'Tell me to put on my sneakers' and she would. This was the only way that I could get going." Whatever it takes, I strongly encourage you to make exercise part of your weekly routine. It will be worth it! And remember: any amount of exercise, even just five minutes, is better than none. Now take a moment and jot down a few forms of exercise you might like to try this week:

_____

_____

_____

_____

2. Go out. Again, although it might be the absolute last thing you feel like doing and you may have to muster all of the energy you have, I strongly encourage you to go out and do something. My patients tell me, nearly without fail, that their depression lifts when they go and do almost anything. Some "outings" that have helped my patients are:

     a. Browsing in a bookstore or craft store

     b. Walking in a park

     c. Going to a movie, concert, or show

     d. Visiting a loved one

     e. Going to church or synagogue

     f. Walking on the beach

     g. Shopping or simply running errands

What might you do to get out and about? Write down any ideas below.

_____

_____

_____

_____

_____

_____

3. Engage in a nurturing self-care activity. By now, you can tell that this is a favorite of mine. If you are feeling depressed, I think it is important to send a clear message to yourself that says, "I am a valuable person. I deserve to be treated well." Treat yourself well by doing something that will make you feel cared for. As I've mentioned, some self-care activities that my patients have found helpful are:

a. Taking a bubble bath or warm shower

b. Watching an uplifting movie

c. Doing yoga

d. Going outside and enjoying nature

e. Painting or doing anything artistic

f. Listening to music or playing an instrument

g. Curling up with a good book

h. Getting a massage, facial, manicure, pedicure, or haircut

i. Buying or picking a bouquet of flowers and making some pretty arrangements

Now, let's pinpoint at least three self-nurturing activities that you could try this week:

_____

_____

_____

_____

_____

4. Join a support group. Many of my patients have found relief from depression by joining a supportive therapy group. You may find great comfort and connection in talking with others who understand your experience. Again, if you would like help in finding a therapist or support group, see page 63 for resources. Also, as previously mentioned, many of my patients have felt greatly supported by online communities they've found at websites such as ObesityHelp.com.

5. Attend to your basic needs. This includes:

> a. *Getting enough sleep.* For most people, this is 7-9 hours per night. If you are struggling to get enough sleep, I encourage you to consult with your doctor. He or she can discuss both traditional and homeopathic options for improving your sleep.

> b. *Eating a healthy diet.* If you are unsure of how to eat in a healthy way following your surgery, I encourage you to speak with a nutritionist. Your surgeon should be able to provide you with referrals.

> c. *Getting some sunlight everyday,* a practice that is associated with enhanced mood. You might try taking a short walk outdoors, having breakfast or morning coffee outside, enjoying a meal outside, or simply sitting out in the garden or on a park bench. If you cannot get outside, I suggest that you consider purchasing a light box, which is a light that simulates sunlight and is used for the treatment of depression and seasonal affective disorder (i.e., depression that occurs during the winter months and is associated with reduced sun exposure).

6. Reach out to a family member, friend, or other loved one for support. If you have specific loved ones to whom you can reach out, write their names below:

_____

_____

_____

As I mentioned earlier, if you aren't able to identify anyone, you're not alone. I have learned that many post-surgery patients struggle with identifying "safe" others to reach out to for support, since they struggle to trust others or "fear being a burden." If you struggle with such feelings, I encourage you to enlist the help of a therapist. He or she can provide support and help you identify safe others with whom to share your feelings.

7. Consider getting a pet. Studies have shown that individuals with pets report greater emotional well-being. If you're open to getting a pet, spend some time researching what type would best fit your lifestyle. Veterinarians, Humane Society volunteers, and other pet owners are great resources in the pet-choosing process. As I mentioned earlier, many of my patients have greatly benefited from the comforting relationships they've developed with their pets.

Okay, now let's make your personal coping card for addressing depression. For this coping card, I'd first like you to identify three strategies from the list above that appeal to you. Then, I'd like you to identify THREE SMALL RELATED goals that you'd like to pursue this week. For example, if you decide that exercise might be helpful, I suggest that you start with a goal like, "Take two short walks this week" rather than "Work out for an hour each day." Another example: if you decide that getting out might be helpful, I recommend a goal like, "Go out twice this week- once to church and once to Borders." Achieving small goals will help you feel empowered- and you can always increase your goals as you see fit! Go ahead and write down your three goals below:

Goals for the week of _____

1. _____

2. _____

3. _____

Now you have three goals to pursue this week to help you cope with depression—terrific work! I'll make space below for you to set small goals for the next several weeks. Don't forget to keep your goals manageable, and remember, if you are experiencing any of the depressive symptoms described at the beginning of this chapter, please consider consulting with a psychologist, family doctor, or psychiatrist.

Goals for the week of _____

1. _____
2. _____
3. _____

Goals for the week of _____

1. _____
2. _____
3. _____

Goals for the week of _____

1. _____
2. _____
3. _____

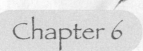

Chapter 6

How to Cope with Identity Confusion

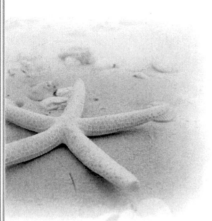

"After the surgery, I suddenly had more opportunities: I could fit in my car to drive, I could wear a bathing suit. This got me asking, 'Who am I?' and 'What do I want to do with my life?' I'd never figured those things out. I never even thought about it. I was too busy just trying to survive everyday. Now that I'm doing more than just surviving, I want to figure out who I really am."

– Ginny

"Who am I?" This is an incredibly common question among my post-surgery patients. Like Ginny, the majority of my patients don't really know themselves because so much of their energy has been spent trying to survive, fit in, seek approval, and avoid punishment. Another patient, Suzanne, described it this way:

"I always looked to my mom for what to wear, what to say, what to eat, what to major in....everything. I hoped if I did everything she wanted, she'd stop criticizing me. She never did. Now I have no idea who I am or how I should be living my life. I really don't know myself and what I like....I don't even know whether I like this jacket I'm wearing."

What Suzanne is talking about is confusion about how to lead an **authentic** life. When I say "authentic life," I'm referring to a life that "feels right" because it reflects one's true self- one's genuine passions, preferences, opinions, wants, and needs.

Let me give another example of a patient's experience of identity confusion or "lack of authenticity." Mandy, who came to see me after her weight loss surgery and recent graduation from nursing school, gave this response when I asked her what she would like to do with her newly-acquired free time:

"I honestly don't know. I never know what to do with myself when I have free time. It gives me anxiety. I guess I should work out. I honestly don't know what I like to do. I've always just eaten and studied."

Do you feel like Ginny, Suzanne, or Mandy? Unsure about your preferences, opinions, wants, needs, and passions? Unaware of what activities give you a sense of joy or contentment? Unclear about what you want and need in a friend or relationship partner? Unsure about "little things" such as what you like to wear or how you'd like to decorate your personal spaces? Unsure about what career is "right" for you? If your answer is "yes" to any or all of these questions, take heart—you are not alone, and although sometimes challenging, the journey of self-discovery is an exciting one, rich with rewards. Now, let's get to work at figuring out who you *really* are.

Coping with Identity Confusion Exercise #1:
Learning from the Past

We can often learn a great deal about our authentic selves by reflecting on what we loved to do as children- i.e., what we loved to do before societal, peer, and family pressures took over and steered our behavior. I love to see the expression on the faces of my patients when I ask them, "What did you love to do as a child?" They generally look confused for a few moments, then smile and tell stories of authentic, fulfilling childhood experiences. Pamela, for example, looked perplexed at first when I asked her this question, then smiled and said,

"I had forgotten about this. I loved to have my Barbie dolls put on plays. I did it everyday. I also loved being in our little school plays in elementary school- I even wrote a play in fifth grade that our class put on. I got away from it in middle school and high school though. That's when I started really overeating. I was putting on weight and was just too self-conscious to try out or get on stage."

From this recollection, we learned that Pamela is a self-described "theater person at heart." We used this self-knowledge to help integrate theater into her current life. She ordered season tickets to a theater company and is working on developing the courage to audition for a community theater production. By exploring the past, another patient rediscovered her love of drawing, while others have reconnected with passions for singing, dancing, making crafts, caring for animals, reading, cooking, biking, hiking, and birdwatching.

Now, let's turn our attention to you: what did you love to do as a child? When, and if, you were told to "go and play," what did you do? Write down any recollections below:

_____

_____

_____

Now, take a few moments and think about how these favorite childhood activities might translate into activities that you could enjoy today. What past loves might you want to rediscover? What activities from your past might give you a sense of joy, contentment, fun, or reward today? Write them down below:

_____

_____

_____

I encourage you to try one (or all) of these activities! Write down something that you'd like to try in the near future:

_____

_____

_____

Coping with Identity Confusion Exercise #2:
Browsing at the Bookstore

A large bookstore, such as Borders or Barnes and Noble, is a wonderful place for those struggling with the "Who am I?" question. To help answer this question, I encourage you to browse the bookstore: give yourself unlimited time to walk slowly through the aisles and simply note what books, magazines, and general subject areas grab your attention. Try not to think- just see where your natural curiosity takes you.

When my patients have done this exercise, many have been surprised at where their authenticity has led them. Suzanne said,

"When I went to Borders, I thought I'd just want to look at magazines, but I found myself in the fitness section looking at yoga books. I've guess I've always been curious about that."

When doing this exercise, other patients have discovered authentic interests in theology, gardening, scrapbooking, science fiction, Sodoku puzzles, jewelry-making, and learning French. As you do this exercise, take notes (either mental or written) on what you find. Write them down below:

_____

_____

_____

Now take a moment to consider how you might pursue the interest(s) you discovered in the bookstore. Some of my patients' "bookstore discoveries" have led them to read the books that caught their attention, sign up for classes, and buy supplies needed to pursue a potential hobby (e.g., gardening, jewelry-making, and scrapbooking supplies). How might you pursue the interest(s) discovered in the bookstore? Write your ideas down below:

_____

_____

_____

_____

Coping with Identity Confusion Exercise #3:
What Does the Real Me Look Like?

I remember being so struck when Suzanne said, "I don't even know whether I like this jacket I'm wearing." Suzanne put into words a phenomenon I'd noted in so many post-surgery patients: a lack of self-knowledge about basic likes and dislikes. As I mentioned earlier, many patients have spent a lifetime adapting to the likes and dislikes of others (e.g., mothers, fathers, teachers, coaches, peers, romantic partners) in order to avoid punishment or win approval. As a result, many have not tuned into their preferences around basic things like:

- What styles and colors of clothes do I like?

- How would I like to wear my hair?

- Do I like makeup? If so, how much and what kind?

- Do I like jewelry? If so, how much and what kind?

The goal of the following exercises is to help you learn to reflect your authentic self through your appearance. Why is this important? Because doing so provides a sense of contentment, genuineness, and empowerment. As Georgine said,

"I always just wore whatever fit- and whatever I could find quickly- in the plus-sized section. I'd hated to shop ever since my mom refused to buy me clothes when I was overweight as a kid. She always bought clothes for my sister though. Now I'm really trying to figure out what I like. It's a little scary, but also exciting and even fun to wear things that are "me" and make me feel pretty."

Does your appearance- such as your clothes, hairstyle, and accessories- reflect your true preferences? Or does it reflect someone else's preferences? Do you present yourself in a way that expresses yourself? Or is your presentation geared to seek approval or avoid punishment? Write down your thoughts below:

_____

_____

_____

If your appearance currently does not reflect your authentic self- and if you're not even sure what that authentic self looks like, I encourage you to try the following exercises:

      a. **Start a "Things I Like Notebook"**- Get some catalogs and magazines (preferably some health-oriented magazines with limited advertisements such as Natural Health) and cut out

The Weight Loss Surgery Coping Companion © Copyright 2010 Tanie Miller Kabala, Ph.D.

pictures of clothes, hairstyles, and accessories that appeal to you. As you look at the magazine, don't think too much- just see where your eye is drawn naturally. What colors do you keep coming back to? What textures, patterns, and styles? Then, tape or paste the pictures into your notebook. These images will help you answer the question "What do I like?" Make your notebook a "work in progress"- continue to paste images in as you come across them! As your notebook unfolds, write down your observations below:

_____

_____

_____

b. **Browse the Department Store**- as with browsing at Borders, take an afternoon and slowly browse the aisles of a large department store (one with many diverse styles of clothing, jewelry, and accessories). Once again, as you browse, simply see what your eye is drawn to and take note of what you find. Are there certain styles, colors, patterns, or textures of clothing that keep catching your eye? Do you find yourself drawn to hats? Scarves? Consider purchasing any items that you feel particularly drawn to, and write your observations down below:

_____

_____

_____

c. **Keep Your Eyes Open**- as you go through your days, simply keep an eye out for styles, colors, patterns, textures, and specific items that catch your attention. Write your observations down below:

_____

_____

_____

_____

Is it difficult for you to determine what you like? If so, please do not be hard on yourself: questioning years of messages about how you "should" present yourself and finding your authentic style is challenging. I encourage you to simply stay diligent in doing the above exercises, and consider working with a therapist. Your authentic preferences will come into focus!

Coping with Identity Confusion Exercise #4: What Do I Love?

Another part of finding your authentic self is determining what you love to surround yourself with. Once you have figured this out, you can use the information to create personal spaces that feel "right." When our personal spaces are filled with colors, patterns, textures, and things that we love, we are filled with feelings of comfort, joy, and authenticity.

As with their clothing choices, many of my patients have never reflected on what they love, instead building their spaces around others' preferences. Think about your personal spaces: Do you like how they look and feel? Are they filled with things that you love? Do you like the colors on your walls? Your furniture? How about your window treatments and wall hangings? Is your space filled with "little things," such as decorative items or photos, that you love? Are you not sure what you love? Write your thoughts below:

_____

_____

_____

If you already feel good in your personal space, great! If not, I encourage you to do the exercises below to help you create spaces that reflect your authentic self. These exercises will help you determine specifically what your personal space should look and feel like.

> a. **Keep Filling Your "Things I Like Notebook"**- This time, get some home decorating magazines and catalogs. As you browse through them, don't think too much- just see what your eye is naturally drawn to. Are there certain colors, textures, patterns, and styles that you keep coming back to? Are there items that you instantly "fall in love with?" Tape or paste the pictures of

these items into your notebook- and consider purchasing any items that you feel strongly drawn to. Remember, your notebook is a "work in progress"- continue to paste images in as you come across them! As your notebook unfolds, write down your observations below:

_____

_____

_____

b. **Browse Home Goods Stores** —Again, take an afternoon and slowly browse the aisles of a large home goods store with many diverse items (e.g., Home Goods, The World Market). Once again, as you browse, simply see what your eye is drawn to and take note of what you find. Write your observations down below, and consider purchasing any items that your feel particularly drawn to:

_____

_____

_____

c. **Think About Places You Have Loved**—Can you think of any homes, restaurants, offices, or stores that have given you a really good feeling? Is there a place where you have thought, "I just love how this looks and feels?" If so, write down below what "felt right" about them:

_____

_____

_____

Now think for a moment: what does this tell you about your authentic preferences? Write your thoughts below:

_____

_____

_____

Coping with Identity Confusion Exercise #5:
WHO Do YOU Like?

Just last week, I was sitting with one of my patients, Ginny, who was talking about a new, potential friend named Kathy. They had just had lunch together, and Ginny wondered aloud if she had made a good impression on Kathy, if she had "talked too much," if she had "said anything stupid," and if she "had anything to offer" the friendship. I asked Ginny if I could interrupt and posed the following question, "So Ginny, what do *you* think of Kathy?"

Ginny fell silent and looked at me rather perplexed. This is the response I get from the majority of patients when I ask them about *their* reactions to a potential friend or relationship partner. I frequently find myself saying, "You are so concerned about what they're thinking of you that you don't give a thought to how you're feeling with *them*." I am not encouraging my patients to be judgmental- I am simply encouraging them to carefully reflect on whether another person's personality, values, interests, wants, and needs *fit* with their personality, values, interests, wants, and needs. I have found that most of my patients do not go through this reflection process. In fact, most have no idea what type of person would be a good, healthy fit for them.

Is your experience like that of Ginny? Are you so busy worrying about what others think of you that you don't reflect on how you feel with them? Have you given any thought to what type of person would be a good fit for you in a friendship or romantic relationship? In other words, do you know what you're looking for? If not, let's figure it out together using the following exercises:

> a. **With Whom Can I be Myself?** Take a few moments and write down the names of people, past and present, with whom you felt you could be yourself, felt comfortable, and/or felt joy:

_____

_____

_____

Now, think about the characteristics of these people: how would you describe them? What are they like? What are their defining characteristics (e.g., kind,

caring, compassionate, fun, loyal, artistic, understanding, thoughtful).
What things are they interested in? How do they spend their time?

_____

_____

_____

The information above gives us valuable information about the type of
person who would likely be a good fit for you- someone who possesses at
least some of the characteristics above. As you meet people, ask yourself:
does he or she possess some of these characteristics? If so, he or she might
just be a good fit!

When determining if someone is a good fit for you, it is also important to
know what characteristics are NOT healthy for you. Let's determine this
using the following exercise:

> b. **With Whom Do I Feel Uncomfortable?**- Take a few moments
> and write down the names of people, past and present, with whom
> you have felt particularly anxious, uncomfortable, or distressed:

_____

_____

_____

Now, think about the characteristics of these people: how would you
describe them? What are they like? What are their defining characteristics?
What things are they interested in? How do they spend their time?

_____

_____

_____

Again, this information helps us understand the type of person who would
likely NOT be a healthy fit for you- someone who possesses at least some of
the characteristics above. As you meet people, ask yourself: does this person
possess some of these characteristics? Is this a healthy fit?

c. **What Do I Want and Need in a Friend?** Vickie answered this question with the following statement, "I want and need someone I can trust, someone fun, a good listener who doesn't judge, someone easy-going, someone who has kids around my kids' age would be nice too, so we have that in common." What do you want and need? Write any thoughts below:

_____

_____

_____

d. **What Do I Want and Need in a Relationship Partner?**
For this question, Aaron said, "I want and need someone kind, caring, and affectionate. Someone who would never be abusive. Someone fun who really values family." What do you want and need in a relationship partner?

_____

_____

_____

Now that you have reflected, perhaps for the first time ever, on YOUR wants, needs, and preferences in relationships, let's take a moment and summarize what you've learned:

The kind of person who would be a good fit for me in a friendship or romantic relationship would be……

_____

_____

_____

Since we've covered so much ground in this chapter, let's take a few moments to help you organize your thoughts. Below, write down any strategies from the last 10 pages that you'd like to use in your quest to discover your authentic self.

_____

_____

_____

_____

Terrific work! My hope is that you are on your way to determining who you are and what you are looking for in relationships!

Before I close this chapter, I would like to briefly address one final element of identity confusion: career dissatisfaction. Many of my post-surgery patients report significant unhappiness with their jobs. Without fail, these patients have shared that they did not pursue their jobs because they were passionate about them. Instead, they took jobs because a parent, teacher, or other authority figure encouraged them to do so; because they thought the money or status of a job would make them happy; or simply because they "didn't know what else to do." The result: jobs that do not fit with the authentic self. Jobs that feel meaningless, boring, and depleting. Jobs that do not inspire.

Are you in such a job? If so, I encourage you to seek the assistance of a career counselor, as career counseling goes beyond the scope of this book. You can seek a career counselor at psychologytoday.com. Also, many colleges and universities offer career counseling to their graduates for a low cost. Finally, you can call local college and university counseling centers and ask for a referral to career counselors in your community.

Chapter 7

How to Cope with the Urge to Overeat

"Even though I know what I "should" do when I'm upset, sometimes I just want to overeat, even though it makes me feel ill."

– Lori

I admire you so much for coming so far in this book. By now, my hope is that you have gained some valuable coping strategies. As you begin using them, please remember that just like Lori, there still might be times when you find yourself upset and compelled to overeat. If you experience this, it is *completely* normal and understandable. Just like it took time to learn to ride a bicycle, it takes time to **practice** and **learn** to cope in new ways-especially if you used an old coping technique, such as eating, for a long time. As you work on integrating your new coping strategies, I implore you to be gentle and compassionate with yourself- treat yourself the same way that you would treat a friend who is making difficult changes!

Now, if you find yourself compelled to overeat, I encourage you to utilize the coping worksheet on the next page. Feel free to copy it as needed.

How to Feed Your Body What it Needs and Avoid Emotional Eating

To feed your body what it needs and avoid emotional eating, walk yourself through the following questions:

QUESTION #1: Am I physiologically hungry or emotionally hungry?
Determine this by scanning your body for signs of physiological hunger, such as a hollow feeling in your stomach, weakness, or dizziness. Also scan for signs of emotional hunger: feelings of sadness, anxiety, anger, boredom, loneliness, or agitation. Do your best to determine the type of hunger you're experiencing.

If the answer to Question #1 is *physiologically* hungry, then ask yourself Question #2:

QUESTION #2: What is my body craving?
Try to determine what food group(s) your body needs right now. Think carefully about the foods listed below- imagine eating them- and ask which ones your body needs in order to feel nourished right now:

- Dairy (e.g., yogurt, cheese)
- Vegetables (e.g., broccoli, carrots, salad)
- Carbohydrates (e.g., bread, cereal, pasta)
- Salty foods (e.g., pretzels)
- Fruits (e.g., oranges, grapes, apples)
- Protein (e.g., meat, nuts, peanut butter)
- Whole grains (e.g., bread, crackers, or cereal)
- Liquids (thirst is often mistaken for hunger)

Bearing in mind any post-surgery dietary restrictions, eat *whatever* your body is craving until you feel *satisfied*. I like to say that you are "satisfied" when you have a sense of fullness, but still could get up and comfortably dance.

Remember, no food is forbidden—eat whatever your body is asking for. As you follow this practice, you will find that you desire a healthy combination of the food groups listed above.

If your answer to Question #1 is *emotionally hungry,* then ask yourself Question #3:

QUESTION #3: What am I feeling and needing emotionally right now?
Are you feeling lonely, anxious, angry, or depressed? Do you need support, connection with others, relaxation, nurturance, or to express your anger? Write your feelings and needs on the following pages.

QUESTION #4: What can I do right now to feel better that does not involve food? Would it help to write in your journal, take a walk, talk to a loved one, watch a movie, or take a bubble bath? Look back at the coping strategies you've developed thus far in our book for guidance and write your ideas on the following pages.

– 56 –

My Journal Page

My Journal Page

I recognize that walking through these steps can feel like a lot of work, both mental and emotional. If you really don't want to overeat, but are simply too exhausted or overwhelmed to use this worksheet, I encourage you to try any of the quick, simple techniques in my COPE strategy:

1. Change your environment: Overeating is often triggered by something or someone in your immediate environment (e.g., the stress of work, the boredom of being home alone, the distress of having had an argument with a family member). Therefore, it is often helpful to change your environment the minute you feel compelled to overeat. Go to a store that you like, take a walk, visit someone, or simply go outside for some fresh air. Breathe, redirect yourself and wait for the feeling to pass- it will.

2. Open up to a friend: Overeating is usually driven by painful or challenging feelings, so if you feel this compulsion, call or visit a safe friend, family member, or other loved one. Consider joining an online forum, such as ObesityHelp.com, where you can seek the support and encouragement of other post-surgery patients. Take these opportunities to vent your feelings and gain support. Again, your feelings will pass.

3. Pray, meditate, or do some breathing exercises: When you feel compelled to overeat, diffuse the energy by stopping what you're doing, going to a quiet place (one of my patients even resorted to going to the bathroom at work), and engaging in a centering activity such as prayer, meditation, or deep breathing. These activities soothe, comfort, and clear the mind- exactly what you need when you're driven to overeat by complex emotions.

4. Exercise: As Amy put it, "The second I felt an urge to eat coming on, I put on my sneakers and started walking." Amy, like many of my patients, found that exercise provided a healthy distraction from the compulsion, released endorphins which improved her mood, cleared her mind, and "made me feel good about myself, instead of bad."

Now, write down the parts of the COPE technique that would likely work best for you:

_____

_____

_____

_____

_____

_____

_____

_____

Great work. Now, you're all prepared to care for yourself when the desire to overeat creeps in!

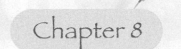

Getting Organized with Your Quick Reference Guide

I truly hope that our work has helped you identify useful strategies for coping with the challenging feelings that often surface following weight loss surgery. Because we've covered so much ground, you might want to take a few moments to create an organized, easy-to-access reference guide- one that you can flip to quickly and easily. You can use the spaces below to transfer the strategies that you identified in each chapter.

My strategies for coping with loneliness (page 14):

_____

_____

_____

_____

_____

My strategies for coping with anger (page 23):

_____

_____

_____

_____

_____

My strategies for coping with anxiety (page 33):

_____

_____

_____

_____

My strategies for coping with depression (page 40):

_____

_____

_____

_____

My strategies for coping with identity confusion (pages 53):

_____

_____

_____

_____

My strategies for coping with the urge to overeat (pages 57, 58, and 60):

_____

_____

_____

_____

Wonderful job! As I said at the beginning of our journey, I'm so glad that you took this important step in self care following your surgery. I truly hope that our work serves you not only in the weeks and months following your surgery, but for a lifetime. Wishing you all the best as you move forward! **Take good care!**

Appendix A: Tips for Finding a Therapist

I'm so glad that you're considering finding a therapist.
Here are some strategies for locating a good therapist near you:

1. Visit Psychologytoday.com.

This web site has a "find a therapist" function which allows you to
type in your zip code and view the profiles of therapists near you.
Profiles include information about each therapist's
therapeutic style, location, fees, and insurances accepted.

2. Ask your surgeon, primary care physician, or OB/GYN for a referral.

Most physicians have the names and numbers
of local therapists readily available.

3. Call a local college or university counseling center and ask for referrals for private practice therapists in the community.

Most college and university counseling centers maintain a
list of local therapists and are happy to provide referrals.

4. Network with family and friends.

If you feel comfortable, ask family members and
friends if they can refer you to a good therapist.

5. Ask your pastor, priest, rabbi, or other spiritual/religious leader for a referral.

Many such leaders keep the names and numbers
of local therapists readily available.

Best of luck to you!

Appendix B: Progressive Muscle Relaxation Script

* * *

The following script can be used anytime you need to relax your body, mind and spirit:

Begin by finding a comfortable position either sitting or lying down. You can change positions at any point during the progressive muscle relaxation exercise to make yourself more comfortable.

Begin by taking a deep breath: breathe in…...hold it for a moment... and now release.   Take three more deep breaths at your own pace, releasing all of your tension as you exhale.

Now continue to breathe naturally for five to ten breaths, allowing your breath to relax you.

Now we'll focus on relaxing the muscles of your body:

Let's start with the large muscles of your legs. Tighten all of the muscles of your legs. Keep holding this tension. Feel how tight and tense the muscles feel. Squeeze your leg muscles even harder. Notice how the muscles want to give up the tension. Hold it for a few moments more.... and now relax, letting all of the tension go. Feel the muscles in your legs relaxing, loosening, going limp. Notice the difference between tension and relaxation in your legs. Enjoy the pleasant feeling of relaxation.

Take three deep breaths.

Now, let's focus on the muscles of your buttocks. Tighten these muscles. Hold the tension….keep holding. Again, notice how the muscles want to give up the tension…and now relax. Let all of the tension go. Enjoy the pleasant feeling of relaxation.

Note the rhythmic pace of your breath.

Let's focus on the muscles of your arms and hands. Tighten your shoulders, upper arms, lower arms, and hands. Make tight fists with your hands. Hold the tension….keep holding…..feel the tension. Hold it for a few moments more…. and now relax, letting all of the tension go. Let the muscles of your shoulders, arms, and hands go loose and limp. Enjoy the feeling as you relax these muscles.

Now, turn your attention to the muscles of your chest and stomach. Tighten these muscles….keep tightening them….hold this tension….notice how the tension feels….and now release. Feel the relaxation. Notice the tension leaving your body.

Next, tighten the muscles of your back. Pull your shoulders back and arch your back slightly as you tense all the muscles along your spine. Hold….keep holding….. feel the tension…..and relax. Let all of the tension go. Note the pleasant difference between tension and relaxation.

Finally, tighten all of the muscles of your face. Close your eyes tightly, scrunch up your nose, and smile widely. Hold this tension in your face….keep holding…. a little tighter now….and relax. Let all of the tension go. Notice the feeling of relaxation in your face.

Now, scan your body. Is there any place that you still feel tension? If so, take a moment to tighten and release that muscle or muscle group. Tighten that muscle…..keep holding….tighten it a little bit more…..and release. Feel the relaxation.

Now, notice how your body feels all over. Notice the heavy, loose, relaxed feeling of your muscles. Enjoy this moment. Notice your calm breathing…. your relaxed body. Take a few more moments just to enjoy this feeling.

When you feel ready, slowly begin to re-awaken your body. Open your eyes, wiggle your toes and fingers, and shrug your shoulders.

Take three more deep, calming breaths.

Your progressive muscle relaxation exercise is now complete.

I hope that this exercise has left you feeling relaxed, refreshed, and rejuvenated!

Made in the USA
Middletown, DE
17 September 2015